Alfred's Basic Piano Library

Piano

Recital Book · Level 2

RECITAL BOOK 2 of Alfred's Basic Piano Library may be assigned after the student has learned *GET AWAY!*, the first piece in LESSON BOOK 2.

The use of this book in conjunction with LESSON BOOK 2 and THEORY BOOK 2 will virtually guarantee that each basic principle introduced at this level will have more than adequate drill and review.

This recital book is coordinated PAGE BY PAGE with LESSON BOOK 2, and is intended to provide a variety of pieces to reinforce all the new principles, concepts, and ideas introduced in the lesson book. The instructions in the upper right hand corner of each piece tell where each piece may be assigned. It is not advisable to give any piece sooner than these references indicate, so as to avoid introducing concepts not yet covered in the lesson material, but any piece may be assigned at any time *after* the student has covered the designated pages.

The authors strongly recommend that each student participate frequently in recitals and other public performances, and these pieces are especially appropriate for such use. Some of the pieces are amusing, and some are more serious; thus they will satisfy a variety of tastes and help to develop the versatility of the student.

The Authors

Willard A. Palmer · Morton Manus · Amanda Vick Lethco

A General MIDI disk is available (8567), which includes a full piano recording and background accompaniment.

Illustrations by David Silverman
(Painted by Cheryl Hennigar)

Third Edition
Copyright © MCMXCV by Alfred Publishing Co., Inc.

2

Use after GET AWAY!,
LESSON BOOK 2 (page 2).

In Spain or in Latin America, any festival or festive celebration is called a *FIESTA*.
Play this with strict rhythm, with even eighth notes, and with a certain pomp and majesty.

Fiesta!

MIDDLE D POSITION

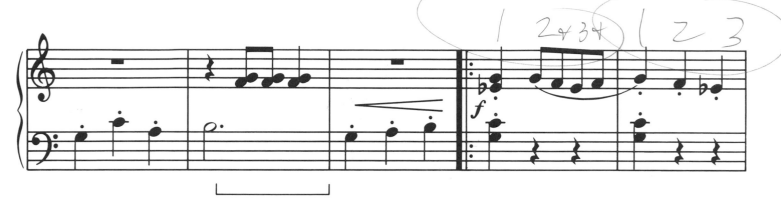

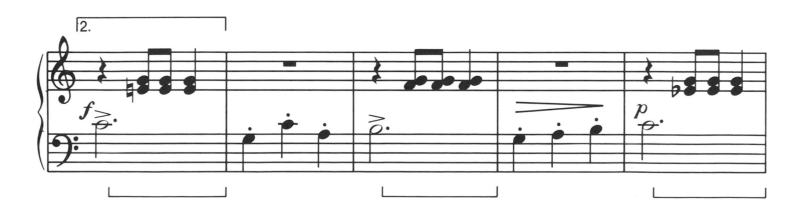

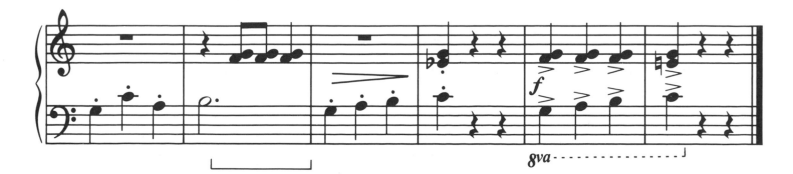

Use after ALOUETTE (page 6)
or ODE TO JOY (page 7).

Toymaker's Dance

C POSITION

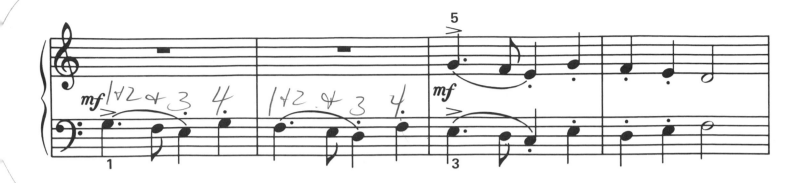

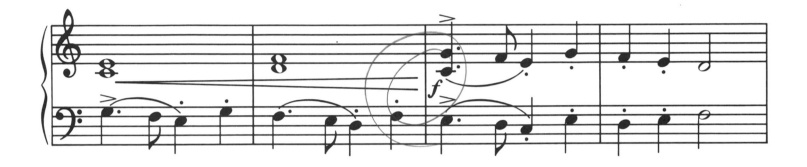

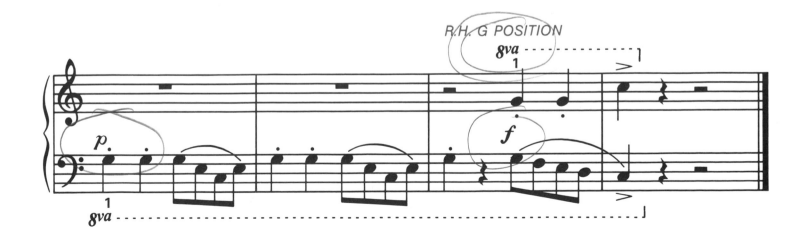

6

Use after LAVENDER'S BLUE (page 9).

Bell Song

Allegro moderato

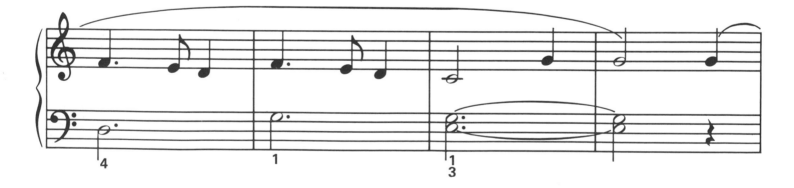

2nd time both hands 8va

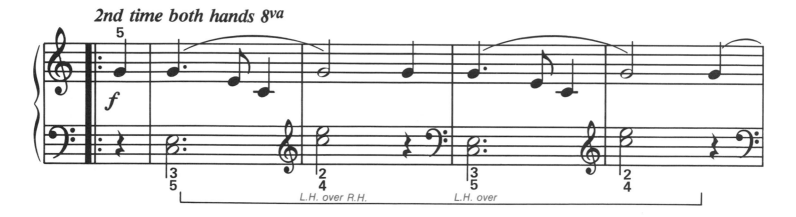

L.H. over R.H.   *L.H. over*

L.H. over R.H.

2nd time ritard.

8

Use after KUM-BA-YAH! (page 11).

Rockin' on 6!

Moderate rock tempo

Rockin' on 6 may also be played with a jazz feel.
Pairs of eighth notes would be played a bit unevenly (long-short).

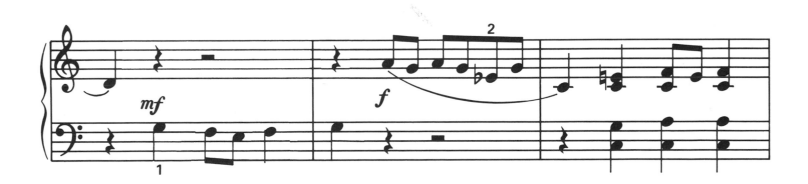

The *Bourrée* (boo-RAY) is an ancient dance originating in France.
It is lively, with two or four beats to the measure,
and always begins on the last quarter of the measure.

A *Musette* is an imitation of a bagpipe.

Use after 18th CENTURY DANCE (page 13).

Bourrée and Musette

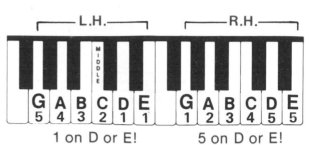

1 on D or E!   5 on D or E!

I. BOURRÉE

Allegro moderato

1st time go to next line.
2nd time go to MUSETTE.
3rd time go to CODA.

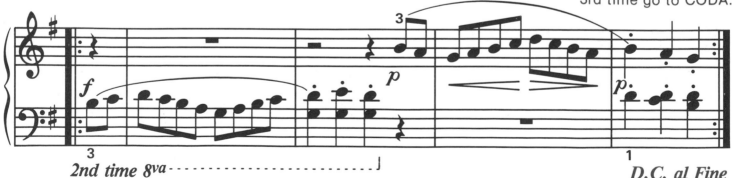

2nd time 8va - - - - - - - - - - - - - - - ⌐

D.C. al Fine
then MUSETTE

II. MUSETTE

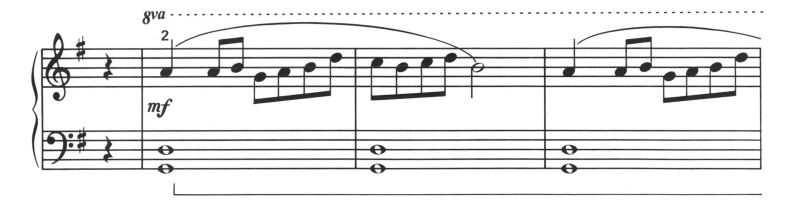

D.C. Bourrée al ⊕
then CODA

CODA (ending)

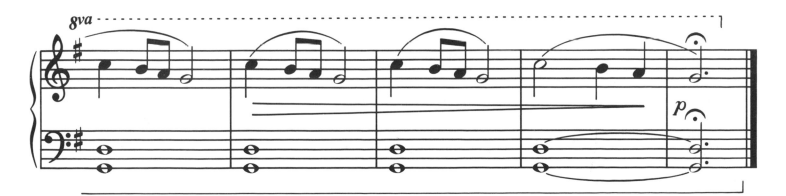

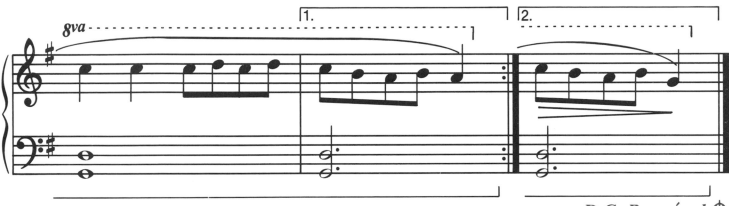

Use after NICK NACK PADDY WACK (page 15).

5 on G or F♯!
2 on C♯!

1 on G or A!

Wash-Day Boogie

Allegro moderato

mf

Pairs of eighth notes may be played long-short, if you wish.

14

Use after LONE STAR WALTZ (page 16).

Come and Dance the Polka!

This piece combines the positions used in *LONDON BRIDGE* with MOVING UP & DOWN THE KEYBOARD IN 6ths.

(L.H. staccato throughout)

2nd time 8va al fine

Fine

Use after MALAGUEÑA (pages 20–21).

Evening Song

Moderato

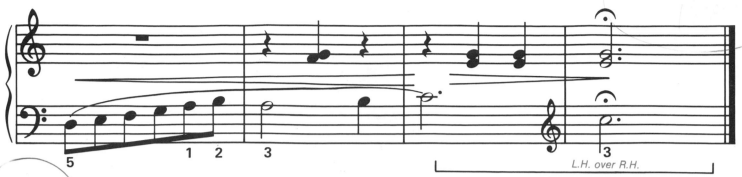

Fine

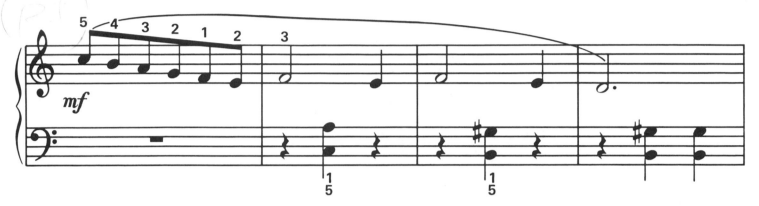

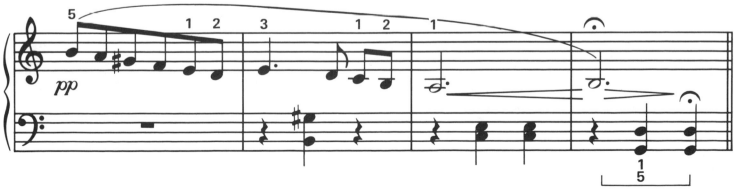

D.C. al Fine

Use after OUR SPECIAL WALTZ (page 23).

Clementine

American Folk Tune

Andante moderato

1. In a cav - ern, in a can - yon, Ex - ca -
2. Light she was and like a feath - er, And her

vat - ing for a mine, Dwelt a min - er, for - ty -
shoes were num - ber nine, Her - ring box - es with - out

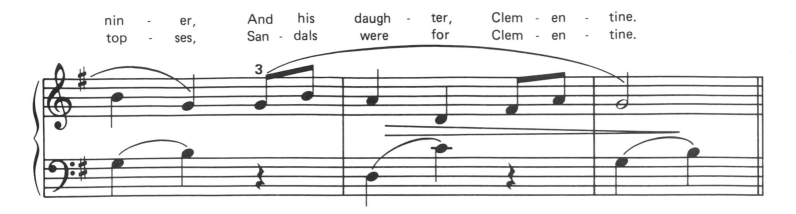

nin - er, And his daugh - ter, Clem - en - tine.
top - ses, San - dals were for Clem - en - tine.

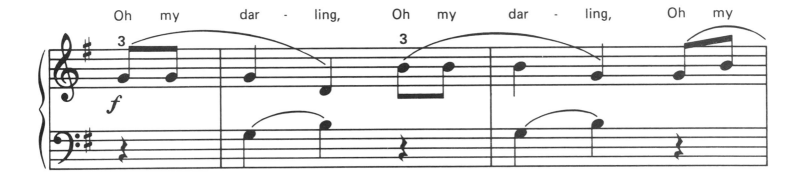

Oh my dar - ling, Oh my dar - ling, Oh my

dar - ling Clem - en - tine! You are lost and gone for -

ev - er, Dread - ful sor - ry, Clem - en - tine!

*Use after PRELUDE (page 25)
or THE CAN-CAN (page 27).*

In TANGOS, all eighth notes are played VERY EVENLY!

Tango Staccato

Andante moderato

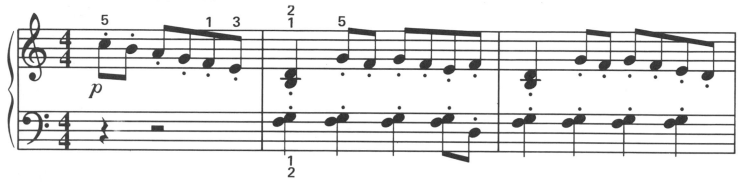

(Both hands staccato
throughout)

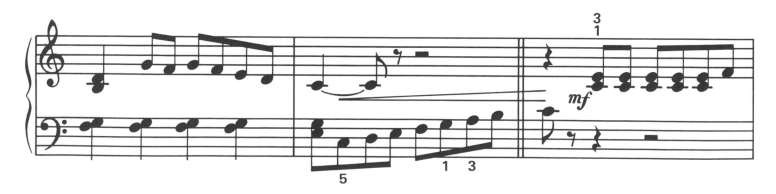

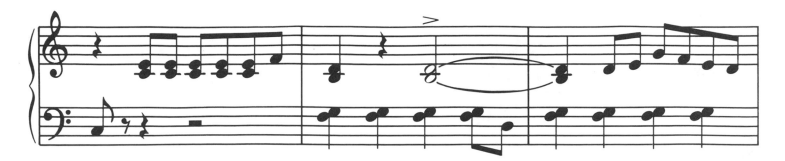

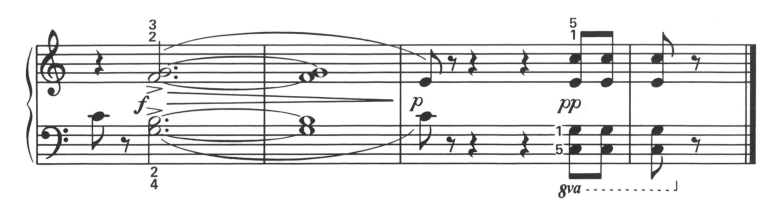

Use after THE GALWAY PIPER (page 29).

Arkansas Traveler

Allegro moderato

American Folk Tune

For an interesting effect, add a C♯ to every chord in the bass clef in measures 1–6.

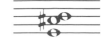

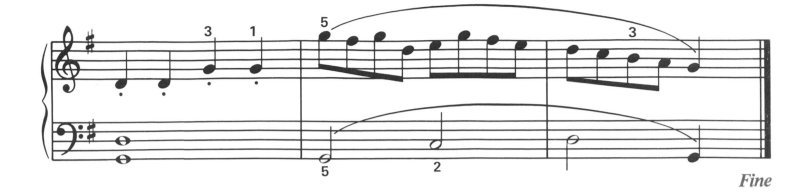

Fine

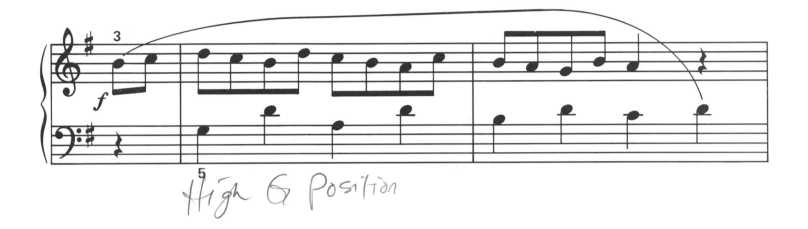

High G Position

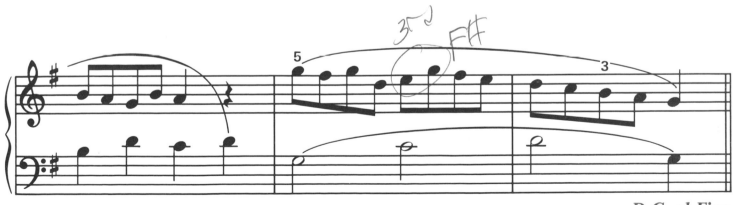

D.C. al Fine

Use after SQUARE DANCE (page 31).

A HOE-DOWN is a lively country fiddle tune usually played for square dances and other group dances.

HOE-DOWN is a complete selection, but it is very effective to add it to *SQUARE DANCE* in LESSON BOOK 2 to make a longer, more elaborate piece:

1. Play ALL of *SQUARE DANCE,* except the last 2 measures.
2. Play ALL of *HOE-DOWN.*
3. End with the last 2 measures of *SQUARE DANCE.*

Hoe-Down!

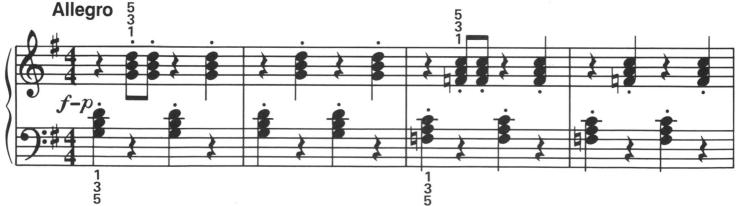

Fine

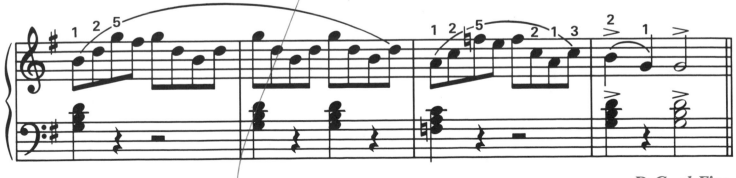

D.C. al Fine

Waltzing Triads

Use after THE PRIMARY TRIADS (page 34).

Allegro moderato

Fine

D.C. al Fine

The Streets of Laredo

Use after GOT LOTSA RHYTHM (page 37).

American Folk Song

Andante moderato

Broken Chords in $\frac{3}{4}$ Time

Use after RED RIVER VALLEY (page 40).

Repeat several times.

Plaisir d'Amour
(The Joy of Love)

This piece was made into a popular song by Elvis Presley. Practice the LH alone before playing hands together.

Giovanni Martini

Adagio moderato
2nd time both hands 8va

*Play the E with 2. Hold it down while changing to 1.

Divertimento in D

Use after OH! SUSANNA! (page 45).

In the Style of Wolfgang Amadeus Mozart

A *DIVERTIMENTO* is a musical "diversion," or recreational piece, usually in classical style. This form was very popular in the eighteenth century. Some of Mozart's pieces using this title have as many as five movements.

Willard A. Palmer

Use after SARASPONDA (page 46).

A RONDO has at least 3 sections. The 1st section is repeated after each of the other sections, and there is often a CODA (added ending).

In this RONDO, the form is A B A C A, then CODA.

Rondo

1st SECTION | **A**

Allegro moderato

2nd SECTION | **B**

Repeat 1st SECTION,
then play 3rd SECTION!

3rd SECTION | **C**

Repeat 1st SECTION,
then play CODA!

CODA